IMPORTAI

MONTH:

NOTES & REMINDERS

PROPERTY INSPECTION
Checklist

EXTERIOR CONDITION: GOOD   OK   BAD   **NOTES:**

EXTERIOR OF PROPERTY

FRONT DOOR

PORCH/DECK/PATIO

DRIVEWAY

GARAGE DOORS

OUTDOOR LIGHTING

PAINT & TRIM

WINDOWS

WALKWAY

ROOF CONDITION: GOOD   OK   BAD   **NOTES:**

CHIMNEY

GUTTERS & DOWNSPOUTS

SOFITS & FASCIA

YEAR ROOF WAS
REPLACED:

GARAGE CONDITION: GOOD   OK   BAD   **NOTES:**

CEILING

DOORS

FLOORS & WALLS

YEAR DOOR
OPENERS WERE
REPLACED:

YARD CONDITION: GOOD   OK   BAD   **NOTES:**

DRAINAGE

FENCES & GATES

RETAINING WALL

SPRINKLER SYSTEM

PROPERTY INSPECTION
Checklist

OTHER IMPORTANT AREAS:	GOOD	OK	BAD	NOTES:
FOUNDATION				
MASONRY VENEERS				
EXTERIOR PAINT				
STORM WINDOWS				
PLUMBING				
ELECTRICAL OUTLETS				
FLOORING IN ROOMS				
WOOD TRIM				
FIREPLACE				

KITCHEN CONDITION:	GOOD	OK	BAD	NOTES:
WORKING EXHAUST FAN				
NO LEAKS IN PIPES				
APPLIANCES OPERATE				
OTHER:				

BATHROOM CONDITION:	GOOD	OK	BAD	NOTES:
PROPER DRAINAGE				
NO LEAKS IN PIPES				
CAULKING IN GOOD SHAPE				
TILES ARE SECURE				

MISC:	GOOD	OK	BAD	NOTES:
SMOKE & CARBON DETECTORS				
STAIRWAY TREADS SOLID				
STAIR HANDRAILS INSTALLED				
OTHER:				
OTHER:				
OTHER:				

HOUSE HUNTING *List*

PRICE	ADDRESS	NOTES

HOUSE HUNTING *List*

PRICE	ADDRESS	NOTES

HOUSE HUNTING *List*

PRICE	ADDRESS	NOTES

HOUSE HUNTING *List*

PRICE	ADDRESS	NOTES

HOUSE HUNTING *List*

PRICE	ADDRESS	NOTES

HOUSE HUNTING *List*

PRICE	ADDRESS	NOTES

HOUSE HUNTING *List*

PRICE	ADDRESS	NOTES

HOUSE HUNTING *List*

PRICE	ADDRESS	NOTES

HOUSE HUNTING *List*

PRICE	ADDRESS	NOTES

HOUSE HUNTING *List*

PRICE	ADDRESS	NOTES

HOUSE HUNTING *List*

PRICE	ADDRESS	NOTES

HOUSE HUNTING *List*

PRICE	ADDRESS	NOTES

HOUSE HUNTING
Checklist

HOUSE SCORE:

PROPERTY ADDRESS

ASKING PRICE: PROPERTY TAXES:

LOT SIZE: PROPERTY SIZE:

FINISH: ☐ BRICK ☐ STUCCO   AGE OF PROPERTY:
         ☐ WOOD   ☐ SIDING

NEIGHBORHOOD

DISTANCE TO SCHOOLS: DISTANCE TO WORK:

PUBLIC TRANSPORTATION: MEDICAL:

RECREATION: SHOPPING:

ADDITIONAL INFO: NOTES:

HOUSE HUNTING *Checklist*

DETAILED HOUSE FEATURES:

OF BEDROOMS: # OF BATHROOMS:

BASEMENT: HEATING TYPE:

PROPERTY CHECKLIST:

				NOTES
POOL		BONUS ROOM		
GARAGE		LAUNDRY CHUTE		
FIREPLACE		FENCED YARD		
EN-SUITE		APPLIANCES		
OFFICE		A/C		
DECK		HEAT PUMP		

NOTES

PARKING

CLOSETS

STORAGE

HOUSE HUNTING
Checklist

HOUSE SCORE:

PROPERTY ADDRESS

ASKING PRICE: PROPERTY TAXES:

LOT SIZE: PROPERTY SIZE:

FINISH: ☐ BRICK   ☐ STUCCO   AGE OF PROPERTY:
           ☐ WOOD   ☐ SIDING

NEIGHBORHOOD

DISTANCE TO SCHOOLS: DISTANCE TO WORK:

PUBLIC TRANSPORTATION: MEDICAL:

RECREATION: SHOPPING:

ADDITIONAL INFO: NOTES:

HOUSE HUNTING *Checklist*

DETAILED HOUSE FEATURES:

OF BEDROOMS: # OF BATHROOMS:

BASEMENT: HEATING TYPE:

PROPERTY CHECKLIST:

					NOTES
POOL	☐	BONUS ROOM	☐		
GARAGE	☐	LAUNDRY CHUTE	☐		
FIREPLACE	☐	FENCED YARD	☐		
EN-SUITE	☐	APPLIANCES	☐		
OFFICE	☐	A/C	☐		
DECK	☐	HEAT PUMP	☐		

		NOTES
PARKING	☐	
CLOSETS	☐	
STORAGE	☐	
	☐	
	☐	
	☐	
	☐	
	☐	
	☐	
	☐	

HOUSE HUNTING
Checklist

HOUSE SCORE:

PROPERTY ADDRESS

ASKING PRICE:　　　　　　　PROPERTY TAXES:

LOT SIZE:　　　　　　　　　PROPERTY SIZE:

FINISH:　☐ BRICK　☐ STUCCO
　　　　　☐ WOOD　☐ SIDING　　AGE OF PROPERTY:

NEIGHBORHOOD

DISTANCE TO SCHOOLS:　　　DISTANCE TO WORK:

PUBLIC TRANSPORTATION:　　MEDICAL:

RECREATION:　　　　　　　　SHOPPING:

ADDITIONAL INFO:　　NOTES:

HOUSE HUNTING *Checklist*

DETAILED HOUSE FEATURES:

OF BEDROOMS: # OF BATHROOMS:

BASEMENT: HEATING TYPE:

PROPERTY CHECKLIST:

NOTES

POOL	☐	BONUS ROOM	☐
GARAGE	☐	LAUNDRY CHUTE	☐
FIREPLACE	☐	FENCED YARD	☐
EN-SUITE	☐	APPLIANCES	☐
OFFICE	☐	A/C	☐
DECK	☐	HEAT PUMP	☐

NOTES

PARKING	☐
CLOSETS	☐
STORAGE	☐
	☐
	☐
	☐
	☐
	☐
	☐

HOUSE HUNTING *Checklist*

DETAILED HOUSE FEATURES:

OF BEDROOMS: # OF BATHROOMS:

BASEMENT: HEATING TYPE:

PROPERTY CHECKLIST:

POOL	☐	BONUS ROOM	☐	NOTES
GARAGE	☐	LAUNDRY CHUTE	☐	
FIREPLACE	☐	FENCED YARD	☐	
EN-SUITE	☐	APPLIANCES	☐	
OFFICE	☐	A/C	☐	
DECK	☐	HEAT PUMP	☐	

PARKING	☐	NOTES
CLOSETS	☐	
STORAGE	☐	
	☐	
	☐	
	☐	
	☐	
	☐	
	☐	

HOUSE HUNTING *Checklist*

DETAILED HOUSE FEATURES:

OF BEDROOMS: # OF BATHROOMS:

BASEMENT: HEATING TYPE:

PROPERTY CHECKLIST:

POOL		BONUS ROOM		NOTES
GARAGE		LAUNDRY CHUTE		
FIREPLACE		FENCED YARD		
EN-SUITE		APPLIANCES		
OFFICE		A/C		
DECK		HEAT PUMP		

NOTES

PARKING

CLOSETS

STORAGE

HOUSE HUNTING
Checklist

HOUSE SCORE:

PROPERTY ADDRESS

ASKING PRICE: PROPERTY TAXES:

LOT SIZE: PROPERTY SIZE:

FINISH: ☐ BRICK   ☐ STUCCO   AGE OF PROPERTY:
          ☐ WOOD   ☐ SIDING

NEIGHBORHOOD

DISTANCE TO SCHOOLS: DISTANCE TO WORK:

PUBLIC TRANSPORTATION: MEDICAL:

RECREATION: SHOPPING:

ADDITIONAL INFO: NOTES:

HOUSE HUNTING *Checklist*

DETAILED HOUSE FEATURES:

OF BEDROOMS: # OF BATHROOMS:

BASEMENT: HEATING TYPE:

PROPERTY CHECKLIST:

				NOTES
POOL		BONUS ROOM		
GARAGE		LAUNDRY CHUTE		
FIREPLACE		FENCED YARD		
EN-SUITE		APPLIANCES		
OFFICE		A/C		
DECK		HEAT PUMP		

NOTES

PARKING

CLOSETS

STORAGE

HOUSE HUNTING
Checklist

HOUSE SCORE:

PROPERTY ADDRESS

ASKING PRICE: PROPERTY TAXES:

LOT SIZE: PROPERTY SIZE:

FINISH: ☐ BRICK   ☐ STUCCO
          ☐ WOOD   ☐ SIDING   AGE OF PROPERTY:

NEIGHBORHOOD

DISTANCE TO SCHOOLS: DISTANCE TO WORK:

PUBLIC TRANSPORTATION: MEDICAL:

RECREATION: SHOPPING:

ADDITIONAL INFO: NOTES:

HOUSE HUNTING *Checklist*

DETAILED HOUSE FEATURES:

OF BEDROOMS: # OF BATHROOMS:

BASEMENT: HEATING TYPE:

PROPERTY CHECKLIST:

				NOTES
POOL	☐	BONUS ROOM	☐	
GARAGE	☐	LAUNDRY CHUTE	☐	
FIREPLACE	☐	FENCED YARD	☐	
EN-SUITE	☐	APPLIANCES	☐	
OFFICE	☐	A/C	☐	
DECK	☐	HEAT PUMP	☐	

NOTES

PARKING	☐
CLOSETS	☐
STORAGE	☐
	☐
	☐
	☐
	☐
	☐
	☐
	☐

HOUSE HUNTING *Checklist*

DETAILED HOUSE FEATURES:

OF BEDROOMS: # OF BATHROOMS:

BASEMENT: HEATING TYPE:

PROPERTY CHECKLIST:

				NOTES
POOL	☐	BONUS ROOM	☐	
GARAGE	☐	LAUNDRY CHUTE	☐	
FIREPLACE	☐	FENCED YARD	☐	
EN-SUITE	☐	APPLIANCES	☐	
OFFICE	☐	A/C	☐	
DECK	☐	HEAT PUMP	☐	

		NOTES
PARKING	☐	
CLOSETS	☐	
STORAGE	☐	

HOUSE HUNTING *Checklist*

DETAILED HOUSE FEATURES:

OF BEDROOMS: # OF BATHROOMS:

BASEMENT: HEATING TYPE:

PROPERTY CHECKLIST:

POOL	☐	BONUS ROOM	☐	NOTES
GARAGE	☐	LAUNDRY CHUTE	☐	
FIREPLACE	☐	FENCED YARD	☐	
EN-SUITE	☐	APPLIANCES	☐	
OFFICE	☐	A/C	☐	
DECK	☐	HEAT PUMP	☐	

PARKING	☐	NOTES
CLOSETS	☐	
STORAGE	☐	
	☐	
	☐	
	☐	
	☐	
	☐	
	☐	
	☐	

HOUSE HUNTING *Checklist*

DETAILED HOUSE FEATURES:

OF BEDROOMS: # OF BATHROOMS:

BASEMENT: HEATING TYPE:

PROPERTY CHECKLIST:

					NOTES
POOL	☐	BONUS ROOM	☐		
GARAGE	☐	LAUNDRY CHUTE	☐		
FIREPLACE	☐	FENCED YARD	☐		
EN-SUITE	☐	APPLIANCES	☐		
OFFICE	☐	A/C	☐		
DECK	☐	HEAT PUMP	☐		

NOTES

PARKING	☐
CLOSETS	☐
STORAGE	☐
	☐
	☐
	☐
	☐
	☐
	☐
	☐
	☐

HOUSE HUNTING *Checklist*

DETAILED HOUSE FEATURES:

OF BEDROOMS: # OF BATHROOMS:

BASEMENT: HEATING TYPE:

PROPERTY CHECKLIST:

			NOTES
POOL	☐	BONUS ROOM ☐	
GARAGE	☐	LAUNDRY CHUTE ☐	
FIREPLACE	☐	FENCED YARD ☐	
EN-SUITE	☐	APPLIANCES ☐	
OFFICE	☐	A/C ☐	
DECK	☐	HEAT PUMP ☐	

		NOTES
PARKING	☐	
CLOSETS	☐	
STORAGE	☐	

HOUSE HUNTING *Checklist*

DETAILED HOUSE FEATURES:

OF BEDROOMS: # OF BATHROOMS:

BASEMENT: HEATING TYPE:

PROPERTY CHECKLIST:

					NOTES
POOL	☐	BONUS ROOM	☐		
GARAGE	☐	LAUNDRY CHUTE	☐		
FIREPLACE	☐	FENCED YARD	☐		
EN-SUITE	☐	APPLIANCES	☐		
OFFICE	☐	A/C	☐		
DECK	☐	HEAT PUMP	☐		

		NOTES
PARKING	☐	
CLOSETS	☐	
STORAGE	☐	
	☐	
	☐	
	☐	
	☐	
	☐	
	☐	
	☐	

HOUSE HUNTING *Checklist*

DETAILED HOUSE FEATURES:

OF BEDROOMS: # OF BATHROOMS:

BASEMENT: HEATING TYPE:

PROPERTY CHECKLIST:

				NOTES
POOL	☐	BONUS ROOM	☐	
GARAGE	☐	LAUNDRY CHUTE	☐	
FIREPLACE	☐	FENCED YARD	☐	
EN-SUITE	☐	APPLIANCES	☐	
OFFICE	☐	A/C	☐	
DECK	☐	HEAT PUMP	☐	

		NOTES
PARKING	☐	
CLOSETS	☐	
STORAGE	☐	
	☐	
	☐	
	☐	
	☐	
	☐	
	☐	
	☐	

House Hunting NOTES

BUDGET & *Expenses*

PREVIOUS RESIDENCE

EXPENSES	BUDGET	ACTUAL	DIFFERENCE

NEW RESIDENCE

EXPENSES	BUDGET	ACTUAL	DIFFERENCE

OTHER

EXPENSES	BUDGET	ACTUAL	DIFFERENCE

BUDGET & *Expenses*

PREVIOUS RESIDENCE

EXPENSES	BUDGET	ACTUAL	DIFFERENCE

NEW RESIDENCE

EXPENSES	BUDGET	ACTUAL	DIFFERENCE

OTHER

EXPENSES	BUDGET	ACTUAL	DIFFERENCE

TO DO: *Previous Residence*

DATE:

MOST IMPORTANT

NOTES:

TO DO: *New Residence*

DATE:

MOST IMPORTANT

NOTES:

MOVING DAY *Planner*

PRIORITIES

MOVING DAY TO DO LIST

ORGANIZATION

MOVING DAY SCHEDULE

6 AM

7 AM

8 AM

9 AM

10 AM

11 AM

12 PM

1 PM

2 PM

3 PM

4 PM

5 PM

6 PM

7 PM

8 PM

9 PM

10 PM

11 PM

12 AM

REMINDERS

MOVING DAY *List*

OLD RESIDENCE	NEW RESIDENCE

MOVING DAY *List*

OLD RESIDENCE	NEW RESIDENCE

MOVING DAY *List*

OLD RESIDENCE	NEW RESIDENCE

Packing NOTES

ADDRESS CHANGE
Checklist

UTILITIES:

ELECTRIC

CABLE/SATELLITE

GAS

SECURITY SYSTEM

PHONE

INTERNET

WATER/SEWER

OTHER

OTHER

OTHER

FINANCIAL:

BANK

CREDIT CARD

BANK STATEMENTS

EMPLOYER

INSURANCE

OTHER

OTHER

OTHER

OTHER

OTHER

START/STOP  Utilities

ELECTRIC COMPANY

NAME

PHONE

WEBSITE URL

START DATE

STOP DATE

ACCOUNT NUMBER

CABLE / SATELLITE

NAME

PHONE

WEBSITE URL

START DATE

STOP DATE

ACCOUNT NUMBER

GAS / HEATING COMPANY

NAME

PHONE

WEBSITE URL

START DATE

STOP DATE

ACCOUNT NUMBER

START/STOP *Utilities*

INTERNET PROVIDER

NAME

PHONE

WEBSITE URL

START DATE

STOP DATE

ACCOUNT NUMBER

SECURITY SYSTEM

NAME

PHONE

WEBSITE URL

START DATE

STOP DATE

ACCOUNT NUMBER

OTHER:

NAME

PHONE

WEBSITE URL

START DATE

STOP DATE

ACCOUNT NUMBER

NOTES:

NEW PROVIDER *Contacts*

MEDICAL

FAMILY DOCTOR

NAME:

PHONE:

EMAIL:

ADDRESS:

WEBSITE URL:

DENTIST

NAME:

PHONE:

EMAIL:

ADDRESS:

WEBSITE URL:

PEDIATRICIAN

NAME:

PHONE:

EMAIL:

ADDRESS:

WEBSITE URL:

NOTES

NEW PROVIDER *Contacts*

EDUCATION

SCHOOL #1:

NAME:

PHONE:

EMAIL:

ADDRESS:

WEBSITE URL:

SCHOOL #2:

NAME:

PHONE:

EMAIL:

ADDRESS:

WEBSITE URL:

SCHOOL #3:

NAME:

PHONE:

EMAIL:

ADDRESS:

WEBSITE URL:

NOTES

MOVING DAY *Planner*

6-WEEKS PRIOR

- HIRE A MOVING COMPANY
- KEEP RECEIPTS FOR TAX PURPOSES
- DETERMINE A BUDGET FOR MOVING EXPENSES
- ORGANIZE INVENTORY
- GET PACKING BOXES & LABELS
- PURGE / GIVE AWAY / SELL UNWANTED ITEMS
- CREATE AN INVENTORY SHEET OF ITEMS & BOXES
- RESEARCH SCHOOLS FOR YOUR CHILDREN
- PLAN A GARAGE SALE TO UNLOAD UNWANTED ITEMS

4-WEEKS PRIOR

- CONFIRM DATES WITH MOVING COMPANY
- RESEARCH YOUR NEW COMMUNITY
- START PACKING BOXES
- PURCHASE MOVING INSURANCE
- ORGANIZE FINANCIAL & LEGAL DOCUMENTS IN ONE PLACE
- FIND SNOW REMOVAL OR LANDSCAPE SERVICE FOR NEW RESIDENCE
- RESEARCH NEW DOCTOR, DENTIST, VETERNARIAN, ETC

2-WEEKS PRIOR

- PLAN FOR PET TRANSPORT DURING MOVE
- SET UP MAIL FORWARDING SERVICE
- TRANSFER HOMEOWNERS INSURANCE TO NEW RESIDENCE
- TRANSFER UTILITIES TO NEW RESIDENCE
- UPDATE YOUR DRIVER'S LICENSE

MOVING DAY *Planner*

6-WEEKS PRIOR

- [ ]
- [ ]
- [ ]
- [ ]
- [ ]
- [ ]
- [ ]
- [ ]
- [ ]

4-WEEKS PRIOR

- [ ]
- [ ]
- [ ]
- [ ]
- [ ]
- [ ]
- [ ]

2-WEEKS PRIOR

- [ ]
- [ ]
- [ ]
- [ ]
- [ ]

MOVING DAY *Planner*

WEEK OF MOVE

MOVING DAY

NOTES & REMINDERS

MOVING DAY *Planner*

6-WEEKS PRIOR

4-WEEKS PRIOR

2-WEEKS PRIOR

MOVING DAY *Planner*

WEEK OF MOVE

MOVING DAY

NOTES & REMINDERS

IMPORTANT DATES

Month

Notes

MOVING BOX *Inventory*

ROOM: BOX NO: COLOR CODE:

CONTENTS:

ROOM: BOX NO: COLOR CODE:

CONTENTS:

ROOM: BOX NO: COLOR CODE:

CONTENTS:

ROOM: BOX NO: COLOR CODE:

CONTENTS:

MOVING BOX *Inventory*

ROOM: BOX NO: COLOR CODE:

CONTENTS:

ROOM: BOX NO: COLOR CODE:

CONTENTS:

ROOM: BOX NO: COLOR CODE:

CONTENTS:

ROOM: BOX NO: COLOR CODE:

CONTENTS:

MOVING BOX *Inventory*

ROOM: BOX NO: COLOR CODE:

CONTENTS:

ROOM: BOX NO: COLOR CODE:

CONTENTS:

ROOM: BOX NO: COLOR CODE:

CONTENTS:

ROOM: BOX NO: COLOR CODE:

CONTENTS:

MOVING BOX *Inventory*

ROOM: BOX NO: COLOR CODE:

CONTENTS:

ROOM: BOX NO: COLOR CODE:

CONTENTS:

ROOM: BOX NO: COLOR CODE:

CONTENTS:

ROOM: BOX NO: COLOR CODE:

CONTENTS:

MOVING BOX *Inventory*

ROOM: BOX NO: COLOR CODE:

CONTENTS:

ROOM: BOX NO: COLOR CODE:

CONTENTS:

ROOM: BOX NO: COLOR CODE:

CONTENTS:

ROOM: BOX NO: COLOR CODE:

CONTENTS:

MOVING BOX *Inventory*

ROOM: BOX NO: COLOR CODE:

CONTENTS:

ROOM: BOX NO: COLOR CODE:

CONTENTS:

ROOM: BOX NO: COLOR CODE:

CONTENTS:

ROOM: BOX NO: COLOR CODE:

CONTENTS:

MOVING BOX *Inventory*

ROOM: BOX NO: COLOR CODE:

CONTENTS:

ROOM: BOX NO: COLOR CODE:

CONTENTS:

ROOM: BOX NO: COLOR CODE:

CONTENTS:

ROOM: BOX NO: COLOR CODE:

CONTENTS:

MOVING BOX *Inventory*

ROOM: BOX NO: COLOR CODE:

CONTENTS:

ROOM: BOX NO: COLOR CODE:

CONTENTS:

ROOM: BOX NO: COLOR CODE:

CONTENTS:

ROOM: BOX NO: COLOR CODE:

CONTENTS:

MOVING BOX *Inventory*

ROOM: BOX NO: COLOR CODE:

CONTENTS:

ROOM: BOX NO: COLOR CODE:

CONTENTS:

ROOM: BOX NO: COLOR CODE:

CONTENTS:

ROOM: BOX NO: COLOR CODE:

CONTENTS:

MOVING BOX *Inventory*

ROOM: BOX NO: COLOR CODE:

CONTENTS:

ROOM: BOX NO: COLOR CODE:

CONTENTS:

ROOM: BOX NO: COLOR CODE:

CONTENTS:

ROOM: BOX NO: COLOR CODE:

CONTENTS:

MOVING BOX *Inventory*

ROOM: BOX NO: COLOR CODE:

CONTENTS:

ROOM: BOX NO: COLOR CODE:

CONTENTS:

ROOM: BOX NO: COLOR CODE:

CONTENTS:

ROOM: BOX NO: COLOR CODE:

CONTENTS:

MOVING BOX *Inventory*

ROOM: BOX NO: COLOR CODE:

CONTENTS:

ROOM: BOX NO: COLOR CODE:

CONTENTS:

ROOM: BOX NO: COLOR CODE:

CONTENTS:

ROOM: BOX NO: COLOR CODE:

CONTENTS:

MOVING BOX *Inventory*

ROOM:	BOX NO:	COLOR CODE:

CONTENTS:

ROOM:	BOX NO:	COLOR CODE:

CONTENTS:

ROOM:	BOX NO:	COLOR CODE:

CONTENTS:

ROOM:	BOX NO:	COLOR CODE:

CONTENTS:

MOVING BOX *Inventory*

ROOM: BOX NO: COLOR CODE:

CONTENTS:

ROOM: BOX NO: COLOR CODE:

CONTENTS:

ROOM: BOX NO: COLOR CODE:

CONTENTS:

ROOM: BOX NO: COLOR CODE:

CONTENTS:

MOVING BOX *Inventory*

ROOM: BOX NO: COLOR CODE:

CONTENTS:

ROOM: BOX NO: COLOR CODE:

CONTENTS:

ROOM: BOX NO: COLOR CODE:

CONTENTS:

ROOM: BOX NO: COLOR CODE:

CONTENTS:

MOVING BOX *Inventory*

ROOM: BOX NO: COLOR CODE:

CONTENTS:

ROOM: BOX NO: COLOR CODE:

CONTENTS:

ROOM: BOX NO: COLOR CODE:

CONTENTS:

ROOM: BOX NO: COLOR CODE:

CONTENTS:

MOVING BOX *Inventory*

ROOM: BOX NO: COLOR CODE:

CONTENTS:

ROOM: BOX NO: COLOR CODE:

CONTENTS:

ROOM: BOX NO: COLOR CODE:

CONTENTS:

ROOM: BOX NO: COLOR CODE:

CONTENTS:

MOVING BOX *Inventory*

ROOM: BOX NO: COLOR CODE:

CONTENTS:

ROOM: BOX NO: COLOR CODE:

CONTENTS:

ROOM: BOX NO: COLOR CODE:

CONTENTS:

ROOM: BOX NO: COLOR CODE:

CONTENTS:

MOVING BOX *Inventory*

ROOM: BOX NO: COLOR CODE:

CONTENTS:

ROOM: BOX NO: COLOR CODE:

CONTENTS:

ROOM: BOX NO: COLOR CODE:

CONTENTS:

ROOM: BOX NO: COLOR CODE:

CONTENTS:

MOVING BOX *Inventory*

ROOM: BOX NO: COLOR CODE:

CONTENTS:

ROOM: BOX NO: COLOR CODE:

CONTENTS:

ROOM: BOX NO: COLOR CODE:

CONTENTS:

ROOM: BOX NO: COLOR CODE:

CONTENTS:

MOVING BOX *Inventory*

ROOM: BOX NO: COLOR CODE:

CONTENTS:

ROOM: BOX NO: COLOR CODE:

CONTENTS:

ROOM: BOX NO: COLOR CODE:

CONTENTS:

ROOM: BOX NO: COLOR CODE:

CONTENTS:

MOVING BOX *Inventory*

ROOM: BOX NO: COLOR CODE:

CONTENTS:

ROOM: BOX NO: COLOR CODE:

CONTENTS:

ROOM: BOX NO: COLOR CODE:

CONTENTS:

ROOM: BOX NO: COLOR CODE:

CONTENTS:

MOVING BOX *Inventory*

ROOM: BOX NO: COLOR CODE:

CONTENTS:

ROOM: BOX NO: COLOR CODE:

CONTENTS:

ROOM: BOX NO: COLOR CODE:

CONTENTS:

ROOM: BOX NO: COLOR CODE:

CONTENTS:

MOVING BOX *Inventory*

ROOM: BOX NO: COLOR CODE:

CONTENTS:

ROOM: BOX NO: COLOR CODE:

CONTENTS:

ROOM: BOX NO: COLOR CODE:

CONTENTS:

ROOM: BOX NO: COLOR CODE:

CONTENTS:

MOVING BOX *Inventory*

ROOM: BOX NO: COLOR CODE:

CONTENTS:

ROOM: BOX NO: COLOR CODE:

CONTENTS:

ROOM: BOX NO: COLOR CODE:

CONTENTS:

ROOM: BOX NO: COLOR CODE:

CONTENTS:

MOVING BOX *Inventory*

ROOM: BOX NO: COLOR CODE:

CONTENTS:

ROOM: BOX NO: COLOR CODE:

CONTENTS:

ROOM: BOX NO: COLOR CODE:

CONTENTS:

ROOM: BOX NO: COLOR CODE:

CONTENTS:

MOVING BOX *Inventory*

ROOM: BOX NO: COLOR CODE:

CONTENTS:

ROOM: BOX NO: COLOR CODE:

CONTENTS:

ROOM: BOX NO: COLOR CODE:

CONTENTS:

ROOM: BOX NO: COLOR CODE:

CONTENTS:

MOVING BOX *Inventory*

ROOM: BOX NO: COLOR CODE:

CONTENTS:

ROOM: BOX NO: COLOR CODE:

CONTENTS:

ROOM: BOX NO: COLOR CODE:

CONTENTS:

ROOM: BOX NO: COLOR CODE:

CONTENTS:

MOVING BOX *Inventory*

ROOM: BOX NO: COLOR CODE:

CONTENTS:

ROOM: BOX NO: COLOR CODE:

CONTENTS:

ROOM: BOX NO: COLOR CODE:

CONTENTS:

ROOM: BOX NO: COLOR CODE:

CONTENTS:

MOVING BOX *Inventory*

ROOM: BOX NO: COLOR CODE:

CONTENTS:

ROOM: BOX NO: COLOR CODE:

CONTENTS:

ROOM: BOX NO: COLOR CODE:

CONTENTS:

ROOM: BOX NO: COLOR CODE:

CONTENTS:

MOVING BOX *Inventory*

ROOM: BOX NO: COLOR CODE:

CONTENTS:

ROOM: BOX NO: COLOR CODE:

CONTENTS:

ROOM: BOX NO: COLOR CODE:

CONTENTS:

ROOM: BOX NO: COLOR CODE:

CONTENTS:

MOVING BOX *Inventory*

ROOM: BOX NO: COLOR CODE:

CONTENTS:

ROOM: BOX NO: COLOR CODE:

CONTENTS:

ROOM: BOX NO: COLOR CODE:

CONTENTS:

ROOM: BOX NO: COLOR CODE:

CONTENTS:

MOVING BOX *Inventory*

ROOM: BOX NO: COLOR CODE:

CONTENTS:

ROOM: BOX NO: COLOR CODE:

CONTENTS:

ROOM: BOX NO: COLOR CODE:

CONTENTS:

ROOM: BOX NO: COLOR CODE:

CONTENTS:

MOVING BOX *Inventory*

ROOM: BOX NO: COLOR CODE:

CONTENTS:

ROOM: BOX NO: COLOR CODE:

CONTENTS:

ROOM: BOX NO: COLOR CODE:

CONTENTS:

ROOM: BOX NO: COLOR CODE:

CONTENTS:

ROOM *Planner*

ROOM: KITCHEN

PAINT COLORS::
....

COLOR SCHEME: Green
....

DÉCOR IDEAS:
....

FURNITURE IDEAS:
....

NOTES:

Green subway tiles
....
....
....
....

ROOM: LIVING ROOM

PAINT COLORS::
....

COLOR SCHEME:
....

DÉCOR IDEAS:
....

FURNITURE IDEAS:
....

NOTES:
....
....
....
....
....
....

NEW ROOM *Planner*

ROOM: BEDROOM

PAINT COLORS::

COLOR CODE:

DÉCOR IDEAS:

FURNITURE IDEAS:

THINGS TO DO:

- [ ]
- [ ]
- [ ]
- [ ]
- [ ]
- [ ]
- [ ]
- [ ]
- [ ]
- [ ]
- [ ]

DÉCOR IDEAS:

ROOM *Planner*

ROOM:

PAINT COLORS::

COLOR SCHEME:

DÉCOR IDEAS:

FURNITURE IDEAS:

NOTES:

ROOM:

PAINT COLORS::

COLOR SCHEME:

DÉCOR IDEAS:

FURNITURE IDEAS:

NOTES:

NEW ROOM *Planner*

ROOM:

PAINT COLORS::

COLOR CODE:

DÉCOR IDEAS:

FURNITURE IDEAS:

THINGS TO DO:

- [ ]
- [ ]
- [ ]
- [ ]
- [ ]
- [ ]
- [ ]
- [ ]
- [ ]
- [ ]
- [ ]

DÉCOR IDEAS:

ROOM *Planner*

ROOM:

PAINT COLORS::

COLOR SCHEME:

DÉCOR IDEAS:

FURNITURE IDEAS:

NOTES:

ROOM:

PAINT COLORS::

COLOR SCHEME:

DÉCOR IDEAS:

FURNITURE IDEAS:

NOTES:

NEW ROOM *Planner*

ROOM:

PAINT COLORS::

COLOR CODE:

DÉCOR IDEAS:

FURNITURE IDEAS:

THINGS TO DO:

- [ ]
- [ ]
- [ ]
- [ ]
- [ ]
- [ ]
- [ ]
- [ ]
- [ ]
- [ ]
- [ ]

DÉCOR IDEAS:

ROOM *Planner*

ROOM:

PAINT COLORS::

COLOR SCHEME:

DÉCOR IDEAS:

FURNITURE IDEAS:

NOTES:

ROOM:

PAINT COLORS::

COLOR SCHEME:

DÉCOR IDEAS:

FURNITURE IDEAS:

NOTES:

NEW ROOM *Planner*

ROOM:

PAINT COLORS::

COLOR CODE:

DÉCOR IDEAS:

FURNITURE IDEAS:

THINGS TO DO:

- [ ]
- [ ]
- [ ]
- [ ]
- [ ]
- [ ]
- [ ]
- [ ]
- [ ]
- [ ]
- [ ]

DÉCOR IDEAS:

ROOM *Planner*

ROOM:

PAINT COLORS::

COLOR SCHEME:

DÉCOR IDEAS:

FURNITURE IDEAS:

NOTES:

ROOM:

PAINT COLORS::

COLOR SCHEME:

DÉCOR IDEAS:

FURNITURE IDEAS:

NOTES:

NEW ROOM *Planner*

ROOM:

PAINT COLORS::

COLOR CODE:

DÉCOR IDEAS:

FURNITURE IDEAS:

THINGS TO DO:

- [ ]
- [ ]
- [ ]
- [ ]
- [ ]
- [ ]
- [ ]
- [ ]
- [ ]
- [ ]
- [ ]

DÉCOR IDEAS:

ROOM *Planner*

ROOM:

PAINT COLORS::

COLOR SCHEME:

DÉCOR IDEAS:

FURNITURE IDEAS:

NOTES:

ROOM:

PAINT COLORS::

COLOR SCHEME:

DÉCOR IDEAS:

FURNITURE IDEAS:

NOTES:

NEW ROOM *Planner*

ROOM:

PAINT COLORS::

COLOR CODE:

DÉCOR IDEAS:

FURNITURE IDEAS:

THINGS TO DO:

- [ ]
- [ ]
- [ ]
- [ ]
- [ ]
- [ ]
- [ ]
- [ ]
- [ ]
- [ ]
- [ ]

DÉCOR IDEAS:

ROOM *Planner*

ROOM:

PAINT COLORS::

COLOR SCHEME:

DÉCOR IDEAS:

FURNITURE IDEAS:

NOTES:

ROOM:

PAINT COLORS::

COLOR SCHEME:

DÉCOR IDEAS:

FURNITURE IDEAS:

NOTES:

NEW ROOM *Planner*

ROOM:

PAINT COLORS::

COLOR CODE:

DÉCOR IDEAS:

FURNITURE IDEAS:

THINGS TO DO:

- [ ]
- [ ]
- [ ]
- [ ]
- [ ]
- [ ]
- [ ]
- [ ]
- [ ]
- [ ]

DÉCOR IDEAS:

NEW ROOM *Planner*

ROOM:

PAINT COLORS::

COLOR CODE:

DÉCOR IDEAS:

FURNITURE IDEAS:

THINGS TO DO:

- [ ]
- [ ]
- [ ]
- [ ]
- [ ]
- [ ]
- [ ]
- [ ]
- [ ]
- [ ]
- [ ]

DÉCOR IDEAS:

NEW ROOM *Planner*

ROOM:

PAINT COLORS::

COLOR CODE:

DÉCOR IDEAS:

FURNITURE IDEAS:

THINGS TO DO:

- [ ]
- [ ]
- [ ]
- [ ]
- [ ]
- [ ]
- [ ]
- [ ]
- [ ]
- [ ]
- [ ]

DÉCOR IDEAS:

NEW ROOM *Planner*

ROOM:

PAINT COLORS::

COLOR CODE:

DÉCOR IDEAS:

FURNITURE IDEAS:

THINGS TO DO:

- [ ]
- [ ]
- [ ]
- [ ]
- [ ]
- [ ]
- [ ]
- [ ]
- [ ]
- [ ]

DÉCOR IDEAS:

NEW ROOM *Planner*

ROOM:

PAINT COLORS::

COLOR CODE:

DÉCOR IDEAS:

FURNITURE IDEAS:

THINGS TO DO:

- [ ]
- [ ]
- [ ]
- [ ]
- [ ]
- [ ]
- [ ]
- [ ]
- [ ]
- [ ]
- [ ]

DÉCOR IDEAS:

ROOM *Planner*

ROOM:

PAINT COLORS::

COLOR SCHEME:

DÉCOR IDEAS:

FURNITURE IDEAS:

NOTES:

ROOM:

PAINT COLORS::

COLOR SCHEME:

DÉCOR IDEAS:

FURNITURE IDEAS:

NOTES:

NEW ROOM *Planner*

ROOM:

PAINT COLORS::

COLOR CODE:

DÉCOR IDEAS:

FURNITURE IDEAS:

THINGS TO DO:

- [ ]
- [ ]
- [ ]
- [ ]
- [ ]
- [ ]
- [ ]
- [ ]
- [ ]
- [ ]

DÉCOR IDEAS:

ROOM *Planner*

ROOM:

PAINT COLORS::

COLOR SCHEME:

DÉCOR IDEAS:

FURNITURE IDEAS:

NOTES:

ROOM:

PAINT COLORS::

COLOR SCHEME:

DÉCOR IDEAS:

FURNITURE IDEAS:

NOTES:

ROOM *Planner*

ROOM:

PAINT COLORS::

COLOR SCHEME:

DÉCOR IDEAS:

FURNITURE IDEAS:

NOTES:

ROOM:

PAINT COLORS::

COLOR SCHEME:

DÉCOR IDEAS:

FURNITURE IDEAS:

NOTES:

NEW ROOM *Planner*

ROOM:

PAINT COLORS::

COLOR CODE:

DÉCOR IDEAS:

FURNITURE IDEAS:

THINGS TO DO:

- [ ]
- [ ]
- [ ]
- [ ]
- [ ]
- [ ]
- [ ]
- [ ]
- [ ]
- [ ]
- [ ]

DÉCOR IDEAS:

NEW ROOM *Planner*

ROOM:

PAINT COLORS::

COLOR CODE:

DÉCOR IDEAS:

FURNITURE IDEAS:

THINGS TO DO:

- [ ]
- [ ]
- [ ]
- [ ]
- [ ]
- [ ]
- [ ]
- [ ]
- [ ]
- [ ]
- [ ]

DÉCOR IDEAS:

NEW ROOM *Planner*

ROOM:

PAINT COLORS::

COLOR CODE:

DÉCOR IDEAS:

FURNITURE IDEAS:

THINGS TO DO:

- [ ]
- [ ]
- [ ]
- [ ]
- [ ]
- [ ]
- [ ]
- [ ]
- [ ]
- [ ]
- [ ]

DÉCOR IDEAS:

ROOM *Planner*

ROOM:

PAINT COLORS::

COLOR SCHEME:

DÉCOR IDEAS:

FURNITURE IDEAS:

NOTES:

ROOM:

PAINT COLORS::

COLOR SCHEME:

DÉCOR IDEAS:

FURNITURE IDEAS:

NOTES:

NEW ROOM *Planner*

ROOM:

PAINT COLORS::

COLOR CODE:

DÉCOR IDEAS:

FURNITURE IDEAS:

THINGS TO DO:

- [ ]
- [ ]
- [ ]
- [ ]
- [ ]
- [ ]
- [ ]
- [ ]
- [ ]
- [ ]
- [ ]

DÉCOR IDEAS:

House Hunting NOTES

Printed in Great Britain
by Amazon

56312257R00071